Poverty in the Land of Riches—South Africa

Poverty in the Land of Riches—South Africa

Matsime Simon Mohapi

To order additional copies of this book, contact:
Xlibris Corporation
0-800-644-6988
www.XlibrisPublishing.co.uk
Orders@XlibrisPublishing.co.uk
302483

CONTENTS

This book is dedicated to the ten hundred thousands of South Africans who continue to suffer the oppression of poverty and injustice in the new South Africa. It is also dedicated to the millions of the people in the world who continue to suffer the oppression of one by the other.

AUTHOR'S NOTE

This book is a mirror which offers the people of South Africa and their Government a rare opportunity to look at their reflections in totality and then make right what is wrong.

This book is a magnifying glass which attempts to bring into vividness our obscure image so that we should know ourselves better and better deal with our imperfections.

This book is to declare that our government is good and is the government of the people but is somehow strangely entrapped by the euphemisms for racist policies and principles which serve and advance the interests of minority at the expense of majority, making envisaged equal opportunity and justice a myth.

This book attempts to offer the people of South Africa and their government a road towards breaking the unbroken chains of colonisation and apartheid. It is again aimed at stopping exploitation and pulverisation of the multitudes of Black people by the rich and powerful.

INTRODUCTION

I write against legalisation of injustice across government spheres and departments and private entities in our beloved country South Africa. Legalisation of injustice happens when those in the positions of power and influence daily choose to go against the Constitution of RSA in order to unfairly disadvantage a person or group, or advantage one person or group at the expense of another.

Favouritism is injustice. Victimisation is injustice.
Poverty is injustice.

How can injustice be made legal? Something becomes legal only if it is permitted. People permit injustice, by choosing not to speak out and not to act against it; out of fear of risking their jobs or becoming victims themselves.

Therefore in order for injustice to survive two parties are needed; the primary ignorant and the secondary ignorant. The primary one in acting ignores the Constitution of RSA and the secondary one ignores the acting of injustice. What makes them the same is that they both ignore the victim or victims of their ignorance.

Thus injustice to thrive
Needs whole lot of ignorant people
At the upper levels and at the lower levels
Pushing injustice

All are guilty. Ignorance of the law is not innocence.
All are guilty. Ignorance of the law is not an excuse.

Injustice is a sin. It is ungodly. It is evil. Like virus it eats both the primary ignorant and the secondary ignorant. It drains their peace. It squeezes out the juice of life out of the victims. All of us somehow suffer from this injustice.

People of South Africa
Let's stand up against injustice
Let's speak out against injustice
Let's act against injustice
Before South Africa becomes our once
Beloved country; before it is too late
God bless South Africa; Guard her children; Guide her rulers and Give her peace; In the name of all peace and justice loving people who came before us. Amen.

Matsime Simon Mohapi 2011/03/03

DEFINING THE ENEMY
OF THE PEOPLE

Before 1994 South Africa was practicing a vicious system of oppression. The divisions were clear and vivid. The enemy of the people was well defined and clear. The colours were clear and bright. It was white against black. All the afflictions and sufferings of the people—apartheid was blamed.

Now let us look back at the history of our people from 1994. We are today in the democratic reign of the fourth democratic president of democratic RSA. There are no divisions. There is no apartheid. There is no white against black or black against white. There is no colour.

But still the great majority of our people has hardship and continues to suffer. There is no apartheid and so who should we point at. Who and what is the common enemy of our people? People are unhappy and confused. They do not know who exactly their enemy is. This in our time is danger.

People are misled and blame one another as they compete for scarce resources. People are at each other's throats as they compete for scarce positions in government departments and in political sphere of government. People are misled to blame the rich for their poverty, to blame even those who struck it by honest means. People are misled to hate and blame foreigners as the cause of their current state of suffering. People are misled to blame the over stressed government for their afflictions. People are misled to hate and blame the present dispensation and to turn against the present government. People are unhappy and confused as they do not know exactly who their enemy is. People are unhappy and confused as they do not know exactly what the causes of their present state of suffering are. They are confused by the results and causes and by the causes and results. The time is now for you and me to make an attempt in defining the enemy of the people.

To help us define the enemy of the people we should start by asking ourselves these questions. What do I believe in? What must I fight for and what must I fight against?

And this I believe: that each and every individual person should be enabled by the government to become the very best God created him/her to be.

And this I shall fight for: the freedom of an individual from fear, hate, and poverty.

And this I must fight against: any idea, religion, system, or government which disadvantages the individual and condemns him/her to legalised fear, hate, and poverty and makes him/her less than what God intended him/her to become.

Remember that fear, hatred and poverty comes with the type of governments and systems people are born into or happen to find themselves in.

Children are born without hatred. God created us free from hatred because God is love. We are creatures of love. We were born with the God given right to be happy because out of love flows happiness.

Even if you do not believe in God, what remains is the fact that you were born out of love. Out of love making you were conceived. You are a creature of love. So you were born with the right to love. The inalienable right to be happy is God given also to you.

Fear is not of God. Children are born without fear and insecurity. Fear and insecurity develops in them as they find themselves born into poverty stricken families; where scarcity and lack are the order of their lives; where at an early age are confronted with the torture of hunger and worry of where the next meal shall come from. It is here where the right to be free from torture and fear is stolen before the age of five.

Poverty steals away these birth rights from our people and replaces them with fear and hatred. A child with the burning fires of hunger in his/her tummy can not sing. Instead of singing happily, s/he cries in anguish. They grow up to hate life, themselves, and others. Doing crime and drinking and smoking hardest things and doing them excessively are the result of lost love to self, others and life. Inflicting pain against themselves, committing hideous crimes against others, and disturbing the serenity and order of life become the way of their life. And it is rife in poverty stricken families and poverty stricken areas.

People are the only species born with the freedom to choose. God given right to choose. This is the right that separates us from other creatures. This is the very right that makes us human; it is also stolen from poverty stricken peoples. To be born on top of a stinking dump hill gives you no right to choose but to live from it and eat from it and stink like it and die on it. They can not choose to eat a fresh warm pie or sandwich for breakfast but soiled bread from the dumping site. They can not choose to live at the place of their choice because of poverty. Poverty forces our people to live in the worst uninhabitable places. They are disabled to exercise many of their rights because of poverty.

So without fear of any contradiction and in the knowledge that none dares contest my assertion I declare that poverty is our people's enemy number one.

WHAT IS POVERTY?

Poverty is to wake up early in a winter morning, in a democratic South Africa, and travel 57 kilometers in the back of open Toyota Hilux Raider 4x4, doing 100 km/h, on a gravel bumpy road, to consult the doctor in a neighbouring small town.

Poverty is when arriving in town your quivering little boy stammers: 'Mama, I wish I was that dog so that I could travel enjoying the warmth of the heater in the front seat next to your owner'.

Poverty is to spend the whole day outside doctor's rooms waiting for your owner to come back and take you home. Your body is tired and demands sleep. The doctor's medication and injection also demand that you must sleep. And you can not sleep; waiting, for the whole day; waiting

THE SON AND THE SUN

Waiting, for the whole day, waiting
Waiting, for my owner, waiting
Bound by the system and waiting
In shackles you can't see and waiting
In shackles you can only feel the paining
Waiting, waiting, and waiting
The sun can not do the waiting
My son can not do the waiting
Thirteen double zero houring
'Mama I am hungry, dead hungering'
Wait my son, *butle moratioa,*—waiting
'Mama I am hungry, dead hungering'
Butle hle moratioa, please do the waiting

Waiting and waiting and waiting
'Mama tell that to the hunger in me
Tell it to stop its burning fires in me
So that it can do the waiting'
Son, hunger and thirst—no postponing

My son can not do the waiting
The sun can not do the waiting
Eighteen double zero houring
Waiting and still waiting
'Mama I am getting cold, cold and shivering'
Night has come my child and no place to sleep
My owner has forgotten us, sleep child sleep
Hunger, fear and hatred overwhelm sleep
We shall do the walking tomorrow son
Tomorrow when the sun is back
But if my son die tonight
Tomorrow when the sun is gone and back
Tomorrow the son shall be gone and gone

Poverty is to wake up at 03h30 in winter or summer and arrive at the offices of government social services at 05h00 to find the queue of about hundred people waiting. Poverty is to queue and wait for the offices to open at 08h00. Poverty is as the social worker comes your way silently counting people one by one on the queue at 09h00 she suddenly stops before your count and turns you back because they can only help a certain fixed number per day and again because you are lazy to wake up on time and again because you are lazy to look for work. "You people are lazy and do not want to work" she concludes.

"Madam could you please give us that fixed number that you can only take per day so that tomorrow morning we can count by ourselves and not wait for 09h00" a beautiful young lady pleads.

"You think you know too much" the ill schooled one shoots.

"I know very little madam, see I don't even know your daily fixed number," the girl of beauty humbling herself with a beautiful smile.

"You shall regret it", she concludes and turns back to walk away.

After totally disappearing into her air conditioned comfortable office people start talking.

"The way she speaks and conducts herself you may think that she is not Black and one of us"

"I sympathise for the little girl because I know that she shall be victimised. She will come and make applications and go to courts for declarations and all. After all that hundred and one hurdles the social worker shall say go home and wait for the grant; do not call me I will call you. She will go home and wait and wait and wait. Maybe next year after realising that all of us here are getting grants she will come back again."

Poverty is when the little girl must come again next year for the same begging. Poverty is when the little girl must start all over again and go home and wait and wait again.

"You must have changed your cell number and your address; I tried to contact you and searched for you for six months before I gave up. Your applications got lost."

"No Madam, I have not changed my cell number, I have not changed my address, and our mother is still dead. See? Nothing has changed. Only change is our worsened state of poverty, so please, Madam, help me to do reapplication to ease the agony of poverty" says the little girl but this time looking much older as a result of torture from hunger and poverty. The little girl must fight with her emotions not to expose her anger and hatred and hunger and deep fear of running the risk of being victimised to wait the second time around.

This departmental official does not know the cost and meaning of this unnecessary waiting. This unnecessary waiting is a little child who died of hunger. It is a small boy who turned into a street kid. It is a girl who lost her beauty and clutch before time. It is a man who has lost his single state of manhood and died into a *randskaal* and heavy drinking. It is a woman who is forever trying and scraping for something for children to eat. It is the old man who waits for bed and dies on the stone floor of a public hospital. It is the old woman who has no piece of land to bury her husband but instead opens the old grave of a stranger to use for her beloved husband. It is sabotaging the people's government and RSA. It is a nation of beggars.

A NATION OF BEGGARS

A nation of beggars in the making
A nation born without a choice to live
But die every day slowly into begging
A nation born without a choice to work
Without a choice to earn a living
Without a choice to lead a decent life
But condemned to life of indecency
Living from hand to mouth
A life of waiting and waiting and waiting

The month end comes a little grant comes
The mother is faced with extremely
Difficult decision making
It is winter—buy a jersey for the school?
Or buy a pair of school shoes?
What about the food debt at the shop?
Monthly contributions to church?
What if the funeral policy laps again?
I am sick and going from this hardship
But what about my dear twins?
Can not pay the church or the undertaker?
But I will love to have both for my funeral

Oh I forgot about the school trip
The school trip I promised them to pay
To pay this month when the grant comes
The grant has come and there is no money for the trip
This poverty changes people to become liars
Liars in the eyes of their little children
This poverty makes people to become
To become that which they are not
Liars and skunks and alcoholics and little thieves
Little thieves that graduate to become hardened criminals
Hardened and heart lessened criminals
That all South Africa suffers from

Poverty is what you see in the eyes of a Black child in the squatter camp.

Poverty is when there is no food and a child is forced to fill its stomach with water for the night.

Poverty is to switch off a geyser in summer and winter.

Poverty is the bank card at the loan sharks.

Poverty is not seeing places and faces.

Poverty is when you must go and you want to go but cannot go.

Poverty is not what people and freedom fighters fought and died for.

Poverty is to get into a big loan debt and purchase a car which you were better off without it.

Poverty is a little piece of South African land in the hands of our overloaded government.

Poverty is to own a car which every time to drive you must first open the bonnet.

Poverty is to lock sugar away from the lady who looks after your child while you are at work.

Poverty is when your wife packs and goes because you can no longer afford to pay for the house and car installments.

Poverty is when after the court of justice has deducted your salary, you are left with few rand enough only to pay the debt at the tavern next door.

Poverty is not only in the squatter camps, but also in townships and suburbs and towns where water and electricity have been disconnected for months because of inability to pay.

Poverty is the repossession of your car and your house in the suburbs or in town and then you are forced to trek to the squatter camp with broken family, heart, and life. In the squatter camp you automatically qualify to be put on the list of official beggars and the waiting list for "RDP houses". The waiting time is limitless; you may wait for a year or two or five or a decade or even die still waiting.

AGONY AND POVERTY

Agony is to wait and wait
Poverty is to wait and wait
In a public hospital and wait
Wait for the nurse
Wait for the doctor
Wait for medication
Wait for something to eat
Wait for something to drink
Wait for bed to sleep on
And wait and wait and wait

Poverty is to lie down
And die on a cold stone floor
Of a stony place of sadness
Called public hospital
Injustice is the vacant wards
And vacant beds in White hospitals
Called private hospitals

Poverty is the excelling Black child who is kicked out from the private school or boarding school because of the inability to pay school fees. The right to get educated in any school of your choice in the new South Africa is also stolen by poverty. The right to free quality education demands money, and lots of it. Many of our freedoms and our rights demands money and you can only exercise them with money, not only money but big money.

Poverty is where there is no justice.

Poverty is to drive "a typical moving shack".

Poverty is to buy land which was never sold.

Poverty is to be disinherited by super power and super force and then the terms of peace and reconciliation demand that you buy back your inheritance at unaffordable high cost.

Poverty is to die but breathe and walk.

Poverty is an orphan who never knew the warmth and sweetness of her parent's love.

Poverty is to die and be buried before time.

Poverty like HIV/ AIDS causes countless deaths.

Poverty is the fear and insecurity you feel that haunts and forces you to erect the electric fence around your property.

Poverty is uncultured and uncivilized as it forces the man in the squatter camp to use a night pan during the day time.

Poverty is to use an open toilet; a toilet without walls; the 'very most public' private toilet "made in South Africa" for the poor Black people.

Poverty is injustice. Poverty is evil. Poverty is oppression. Poverty is all that is against God and force the people of God eternally to lack, fear and hate.

In the beginning it was never God's intention to create us for pain and suffering but it is all the results of human fault, which is upon human beings to correct. South Africa must repent and turn to God for guidance and wisdom out of this dirty snare entrapping the children of God.

From Genesis 1:26 Then God said: "And now we will make human beings; they will be like us and resemble us. They will have **power** on land, in the oceans, and in the skies." This state of powerlessness on people was never intended by God but it was forced on people by the oppression of one by the other. Verse 29 Then God said: "I have provided all kinds of grain and all kinds of fruit for you to eat . . ." God intended that we should never go hungry and He gave us all kinds of food so that we must have the right to choose what to eat from His abundant providence.

In the New Testament Jesus Christ says that he had come so that we may live life in abundance, live life to the full, not life in poverty, hunger, sickness, hatred, and fear. That is why he cared for the sick; he abundantly fed the hungry, and he instructed the rich to share with the poor. By reading the gospel of Matthew you will come to realise that Jesus of Nazareth, that greatest son of Africa, the son of Joseph and Mary, was the greatest freedom fighter; he fought for freedom from hunger, poverty, sickness, sin, injustice, xenophobia and killings (farm killings), conflict, anger, revenge, fear and hatred. His mission on earth can be summarised in one word: LOVE.

Above all he once said: "This is my commandment: "Love one another".

Against fear in Matthew 10:26 and 28 he says: "So do not be afraid of people. Whatever is now covered will be uncovered, and every secret will be made known. Do not be afraid of those who kill the body but cannot kill the soul; rather be afraid of God".

Against poverty in Matthew 25:35 to 44 he says: "I was hungry you gave me food, naked you clothed me . . ." Against xenophobia he says: "I was a stranger and you received me in your homes". Against revenge in Romans 11:19 he says: "Never take revenge, my friends, but instead let God's anger do it."

Against hunger he says in Matthew 15:32 "I feel sorry for these people because they have nothing to eat. I cannot let them to go without food."

Against war in Romans 11:18 he says:" Do everything possible on your part to live in peace with everybody."

We, the people of South Africa, need God more than ever before and we need to love others as we love ourselves; then, if not all, most of our problems shall be gone. Poverty which millions of the Black people are suffering today in South Africa is the result of injustice. Poverty is Injustice!

WHAT IS INJUSTICE?

Injustice is when after 1994 and even in 2011 and like in 1976 Black children still forced to be taught in "Afrikaans taal". Mathematics, Sciences, Arts, LO and all other subjects are taught in "Afrikaans taal" in schools which refused to transform after 1994. Injustice is when you calculate the enrolment in this school and find Black children to make 91% of total enrolment. Injustice is when in this school you calculate teacher numbers employed and find "Afrikaans" speaking Whites to make 96%. Injustice is when 96% of these children, after completing *Graad 7* in this *Laerskool,* must go to the nearest Secondary School—about 2 km away. In this high school and other 3 neighbouring high schools children are taught all subjects in English. The principal of this nearest High School is always in hot water because learner performance is very poor.

Injustice is when high officials of the Department of Education and union officials who think they know better fail to pick up this injustice and the mill of injustice continues grinding down the Black children.

Injustice is what you get when you visit farm schools and make your own observations.

Injustice is the worker in the private sector and private ownership entities without rights and without workers union.

Injustice is the owner of the private entity who continues to abuse workers without government or any workers union interference as if this private entity is not in South Africa but in another country.

Injustice is the union-over-protected workers in the government departments who come and go as they wish without actually working.

Injustice is the departmental official who get targeted, victimised and dismissed from work for taking a stand against the 'untouchables' for not rendering service.

Injustice is the man and woman behind bars as a result of justice miscarriage carried out by the men and women of the robe who refused to transform after 1994.

Injustice is the injustice suffered by Blacks after 1994 and the perpetrators set scot free by the courts which refused to transform. Black people shot at "mistaken to be monkeys" and dragged fastened to the back of vehicles etc.

Injustice is when you are brought to appear before the man who deeply hates your race and the colour of your skin, and without the desire to listen to you, he summarily sends you to rot in prison.

Injustice is when the man and woman in the seat of power hijack and reverse the gains of democracy and mislead people to blame Councilors and the government.

Injustice is when only those who have connections and friends in high places get jobs.

Injustice is when you are forced to cheat on your spouse in order to get employed.

Injustice is when those who have connections and wealth influence the justice system to be unfair and unjust in balancing the scales of justice.

Injustice is when those in positions of power and influence and wealth steal away your spouse and your marriage ends up in the rocks, and you are left totally powerless and become the laughing stock of the province.

Injustice is a R100-million state-of-the-art new prison few kilometers away from squatter camp built to uproot crime. The new prison complete with sports fields, art, educational, vocational and health facilities. But just a few kilometers away, apartheid's bucket toilet system still line the streets, one bucket toilet per two or three families. Poverty is when children in the squatter camp begin to envy the life behind nearby prison walls; a real show piece as they are told by older children who have already spent days in the Correctional Center. "Inside there you do not have to worry about no drinking water or where your next meal shall come from," they are told as they are recruited to join gangsters and do small crimes. Small crimes grow as they grow to become most horrendous crimes; the very reason why the prison was built in the first place.

Spending money and wasting time and lives in fighting the loosing battle by erecting prisons. Who came with this idea in the first place; to deny people of God given rights and then put them in prison to solve the results of man-made problems? What I know is that the prison system has been around for many centuries and is practiced the world over to fight crime but it gives us social and economic problems in return. Nobody seems to be able to stop this prison system and nobody seems to have sense enough to change it because it fails to accomplish the aim it was built for in the first place.

A man on parole for homicide sums it up like this: "When a group of men take you and lock you up for seven years, it must have some meaning. It must deter you from killing again. But to me this prison system makes no sense at all because I shall kill again to protect my life and my children. The prison has not changed my long held believes on the right to self protection. It only made me strong on my rights and believes."

Injustice is when the schooled and learned and well-read and powerful and influential and rich and overly wealthy see this injustice and poverty but do nothing.

Injustice is when you go to church on Sunday and be told that blessed are the poor because it shall be okay upstairs when they die.

Injustice is to hide away the truth in the interest of false peace and false reconciliation.

Injustice is when people sit and plot against you. Plot for how they can quickly get you dismissed from your job.

Injustice is when the church separates faith and life; the spiritual and the physical, and then mainly concentrates on the spiritual and nothing about your physical wellbeing.

Injustice is, out of envy and jealousy and outstanding paybacks and favours, endless desperate attempts made to get you dismissed from job.

Injustice is when every year you are faced with this or that kind of investigation. Poverty is when your harassment is sustained at the patience of the devil.

Injustice is when you are harassed with endless unfair investigations and unjust suspensions from work.

Injustice is when your seniors and your juniors and your union are part of the same plot against you.

Injustice is when you get suspended or dismissed from your job in government or private entity without union representation or the side of your story being heard.

Injustice is when a people can not choose where to live and what shape and how big or small the house to live in should be.

Injustice is the medical scheme benefits that get exhausted long before end of the year, leading to a situation where you remain uncovered while you continue contributing.

Injustice is when children go to school in the morning but come out the same in the afternoon.

Injustice is when your own union officials join a sabotage to block you from being promoted.

Injustice is when the church divides up a human being and only looks after the well being of the soul.

Injustice is the email, fax, cell phone and telephone of a high official which continue to bar your desperate efforts.

Injustice is to be ignored by those who must help you.

Injustice is when the church in a democratic South Africa continues to discriminate against people based solely on race.

Injustice is when politicians who seek that the question of land and mines be address are shunned and labeled as off the point to the new South Africa.

Injustice is when you get victimised or killed in the fight against injustice and victimisation. Injustice is when your spouse unjustly gets court order, warrant of arrest and successfully gets you behind bars so that s/he can run away with your rival.

Injustice is when people are forced to take less and forced to think that there shall be genuine peace and reconciliation.

Injustice is this in our time that is danger and bottled and thrown away and hope and think that it shall not come up again.

Injustice is when a politician is denied the freedom of a creative thinking mind of the individual and forced to think the same as others. If all the people think the same then no one is really thinking.

Injustice is when a system tries to destroy the free mind of an individual human being, for that is one thing which can by inspection destroy such a system.

Injustice is when a book like this one can not be written and read freely out of fear of being squashed and killed.

Injustice is when the school bus can not transport Black and White learners together to the same school it takes the White learners to. Black learners, standing together with their fellow White learners at the bus stop, forced every morning and afternoon to hike any vehicle to school. White learners waiting for the bus that can not transport their fellow classmates because the colour of their skin is Black. In the new South Africa where people are told that there is no racism and that all people are equal and all is well in the new South Africa.

Injustice is when there is no equality and no equal footing and no equal distribution of land and its wealth.

Injustice is when the Black people are forced to remain dispossessed of their possessions, land and its wealth, after 1652 and 1994.

Injustice is when people are forced to toil and labour almost for no pay.

Injustice is your name in the Credit Bureau for monthly catalogues you did not know you had to pay for or continue paying even after paying up the installment.

Injustice is when you are maintaining and this person demands more than you can afford. She takes you to court and without listening to you the one on the robes screws you double the amount the woman initially demanded.

Injustice is when people are forced to concentrate on *if you die.* Or maybe these private companies know the truth that people are dead without the things that rightly belong to them.

Injustice is when we do not die and they reap high returns and save margins on our death investments and we get no profits.

Injustice is when the church is concentrated on your funeral and wellbeing after death.

Injustice is when you can not live life.

Injustice is the high maintenance court order forced on you.

Injustice is the delayed justice; a court case that is postponed and postponed.

Injustice is when you can not live life in abundance and to the full.

Against imbalance and injustice Dr. Aaron Motsoaledi in the City Press of 10/07/2011 writes: "Before the 1994 democratic dispensation, South Africa had two health systems, a superior one for the minority white population and an inferior one for the majority black population. Our democratic Constitution abolished this madness. However, we have strangely ended up with two systems once again: one for the rich . . . and another for the poor."

With the mind that can see deep into the heart of things, our learned Doctor bravely goes on: "The time has come to save our country from this law of the jungle in which the weak and vulnerable are pulverised by the rich and powerful."

Against imbalance and injustice Psalms 7 in the Holy Bible tells us these about God: "Justice is what you demand, so bring together all the peoples round you, and rule over them from above. God is a righteous judge and always condemns the wicked. I thank the Lord for his justice."

May His will happen on earth as it is in heaven. May His will happen in South Africa according to His justice. May He bring together all the peoples of South Africa and the world round Him and rule over them from above. May His righteousness reign in towns and cities and squatter camps and shanty towns and farms and villages and all over the world. We ask these in the name of our Lord Jesus Christ. Amen.

LEGALISATION OF INJUSTICE

Injustice is made legal when the people in a country and in the world accept the wrong and unjust as normal, permissible and acceptable. For example; in the Son and the Sun. That is a way of life to many in the new South Africa. It happens every day. Hundreds are negatively affected by this injustice. This system teaches farm workers' children that Blacks are inferior to Whites. It teaches them to be less people.

And this is against God and His mission. God's mission is the mission of love. Love one another. "This is my commandment. That you love one another, as I have loved you." (John 15:12)

Love is the answer. God knew it that without love people shall fail and fail His creation. That is why He commanded people to love one another. A big dose of love shall solve the problems the human kind is facing. Because love is caring, kind, patient, listening, understanding, protecting, assisting, and continuously seeking to satisfy one self and others. "Love one another, as I have loved you." That is **God's commandment**.

These accepted and permitted wrongs and injustices that continue to flourish in our country are also against the noble constitution of RSA. Our constitution is good. We, the people of South Africa, are the custodians of our constitution. You should not wait for the injustice to happen to you first before you do something. If it happens to a human being it happens to you because you are a human being. God says: "Love your neighbour as you love yourself." Cosatu says: "An injury to one is an injury to all." Motswana says: *"Motho ke motho ka batho."*

Today you may think that this battle against injustice does not concern you. After the Second World War, in a far away country, they came to deport the Blacks. Japanese said: "Why worry, I am not Black." They came again, this time for the Indians. And still he did not worry. Again they came, this time to deport the Chinese and he began to worry. When lastly they came to deport him, it was too late to act because all who could help him fight this injustice were deported and gone.

So watch out: *"Tshegatshega di ja mme e se re motlhang di jang mmago wa lla."*

CONNECTIONS AND DEPLOYMENT

"For I am not fighting against human beings but against the evil of injustice and of apartheid consequences that continue to squash the Black people"

~Mohapi M.S

Dirty and grubby politics make way into and across all departments and spheres of government. These politics are unjustifiable and unwarranted and they hold back the mission and progress of our government. The noble aims and efforts of our government are sabotaged by the way some people do things, especially those in the seats of power and influence. Their behaviour, conduct and deeds add up to nothing in advancement of the government; but injustice—oppression, self-indulgence, victimisation and favouritism. They are liabilities and danger to the government of South Africa and its people.

These liabilities in our time are danger.

These people hardly ever take other people serious or listen to them. People are sent from pillar to pillar and come out with nothing. I met a man who tried to present his case to the MEC for three months without success. He tried everything from letters, emails, and telephone calls. Lastly he travelled to the MEC's office. He travelled 190 kilometers a single trip to the legislator building and came out without a hearing. We met outside the legislator building in a parking lot.

After talking for sometime and establishing trust, we presented our cases to each other. At the end the elderly man said to me: "If it happens that tomorrow you are in a position of power and influence, listen calmly to the one who pleads. Listen with patience, openness, and desire to understand. Do not stop the pleading man from purging his head of that he has planned to say. Of him who does not listen, the pleading man says 'Oh, doesn't he know that it is not that much that I should win my case; but, a good hearing soothes the heart.'"

The labour federations and unions are very important in the advancement of democracy and in promoting the interests of workers in our country.

I don't know but I have seen some people not working, not delivering service at all, and trusting their all powerful connections and unions.

Let's take a school for an example; the union members in a school somehow can deploy '*these liabilities*' to high positions above the level of the principal of a school. So this man deployed by teachers becomes the Circuit manager or Area manager or District manager or somebody else above. I have seen a principal suffering a continuous sustained harassment and persecution from below and above levels as a result of these connections. I have seen learner's education suffering as a result of these dirty connections. In search of excellence becomes a myth on the face of these dirty connections.

I have seen some teachers coming and going as they wish and the principal totally helpless because these teachers continue to say to the man above the principal: 'Do not forget we deployed you, if you support the principal in acting against us, we shall pull you down as we pushed you up'. So the man above the principal becomes totally helpless and useless; a liability to the government; a tool of abusing power in the hands of these few lazy and uncommitted teachers used effectively to advance their personal interests and hold the education of learners permanently in the state of suffering.

As a result the department of education produces learners who cannot read, write, think and reason at the required level. The level of education continues to drop as lazy teachers continue with misconduct and enjoy double protection of their all powerful union and their connection to the powerful man above the principal.

So the man above the principal does not support the principal because his hands are tied by these dirty connections. As an act of furthering injustice and interests of these few teachers he comes down strongly on the principal accusing him of failing to discipline these teachers (the Untouchables). So the man above summarises the principal and get him dismissed. As a pay back for outstanding price for his deployment, he ignores deputy principals and HODs in this school and other schools, and he promotes this PL1 teacher to PL4, to become a principal. The school moves from bad to worse and every year the quality and standard of education in South Africa deteriorates because of these stinking connections and deployment.

AN OVER-PROTECTED TEACHER/WORKER

A lazy incompetent teacher
Have all answers from the book
Why absent every week?
I have got a right to leave
Disclose the reason of your leave?
I have got a right to privacy
Why so little work?
I teach at learner's pace
Why do you dress untidy?
I have got no dress code
Why do you use improper language?
I have got right to self expression
Why no discipline in your class?
Corporal punishment is banned
Why union matters compromise learners?
I have got a right to association
SGB member asks—why not at school today?
Sorry, it is not a governance matter
But children are suffering—our children
Yes, your children but I do not have a child there

A teacher not working, and going and coming
To that place called public school
To do very little or nothing at all
In advancement of quality public education
A lazy teacher comfortably over protected
By his powerful connections and union
And monthly robbing the government
Of thousands of rand
What a legalised cheating robbing business
Teaching has become!

A FALSE TEACHER

Like bi wheels doing same speed
So are a false teacher and a cheater

Like a cheater who knows good
And do no good
A teacher by mistake
Big mistake for that matter
Knows good and do no good

THE TARGETED PRINCIPAL

Like a target all guns aim at her
Like a dustbin all waste to her
Like an actor on stage
An actor whose part
Is a sad one
To become a principal is nothing
Nothing but to remain being one

Recruitment process of short listing and interviews is nothing but window dressing to cover polluted deployment based on dirty connections. The most experienced, qualified, suitable and capable to deliver quality work is no longer a prerequisite. It is only a requirement on the advertisement and behind closed doors it is who is who to whom.

I also and I personally know the pain and suffering and anguish and loneliness and helplessness and stress and waking up in the hospital as a result of this injustice that continues grinding our people in our government work places.

I mention it so that you may know that I feel lucky and blessed to wake up in the hospital because others you know and I know did not wake up.

I mention it so that you may know that I know what I know that you know or know not, the injustice flourishing in our government spheres and departments.

Instead of becoming a death blow to me, this injustice turned out to be the best thing that ever happened to me because I found my deepest self and being and I also found God and my divine purpose in life. The long months of unjust isolation and banishment into the wilderness from the work place and everyone connected to the department revealed to me my deepest self and the will of God on earth. It gave me a turning point in my life and I quote the words of one great man who said: "It is no longer I who live, but Jesus Christ who lives in me. Motho wa kgale o sule. Mo go nna go phela motho yo mosha Mo gonna go phela ke Jesu." It is then that I started writing this book to help the poor because Jesus Christ says: "If ever you helped the least (the poor), then you have helped me."

And today I do not hate and curse people who perpetrated injustice at my work place as I did before; instead I pray for them and bless them for truly without them my life could have been a total waste and a futile existence. And now I know the meaning of those words in a Sesotho hymn which goes: "*Se beng se le thata se tla nkatametsa ho Morena*". It means that the worst trials can become the sweetest blessings to you and an opportunity to discover God and your purpose in life.

It also gave me time to visit different courts of law in different provinces to see the justice machine in full swing but I came back sick and deeply hurt after observing that our people are still suffering gross victimisation and injustice. It is said the miscarriage of justice. That is euphemism; I say NO, it is injustice in the house of justice.

In the first place it was a big mistake to expect that racists Whites, who were the corner stones and foundations and founders and fountains and beneficiaries of apartheid could change over night and become Nelson Mandela and work against racist's apartheid the next day.

After coming to power in 1948 the apartheid government removed English men from most positions of power and influence and it further removed any one who was thought to resist apartheid and its racist laws.

I have seen people and I have heard of people being frustrated left and right with dockets getting lost, undue warrants of arrest, unlawful arrests, dropped cases, deliberate protracted cases, unwarranted court orders, garnish orders and unjust repossessions.

I know of many cases of injustice in the courts of law and I have personally suffered in some of them. For example, in one case the messenger of court failed to locate me or my work place within 10 kilometer radius of court. He failed for three months and I ended up being punished for defiance of court and heavily garnished thousands of rand. I ended up paying triple the money I loaned from the loan sharks. It was very painful.

One other case. In 2006 my cattle got stolen. I drove around and around in search of them. And believe it or not, I found them loaded on the back of a truck parking next to the main road. I blocked the road to prevent the thieves from escaping with my cattle. I was trembling with rage and my wife who happened to be with me at that odd time called the police. Thanks, the police came quickly with sirens and blue lamps and in high speed. They really made a good impression on me.

After questioning we drove to the police station and statements were written and arrests made and the truck still loading my cattle impounded. During the same night the big owner of the truck and a corrupt police official came to offer me thousands of rand so that I should drop the case. I said it was by the grace of God that I found my cattle and so my God shall definitely be angry with me if I take the bribe money. So I refused to take the bribe money and opted for the search of justice.

In the morning high police officials, I was told, who deal with stock theft, came and photos were taken and my cattle were given back to me. My mother and my wife were proud of me for refusing to take the bribe. But my opened case—it strangely closed or died out. I do not know and nobody seems to know what happened of it. I tried to follow it up and I got frustrated and aggrieved and discouraged and I gave up. And my friend used to tease me and said I should have taken 'the lotto money' and forgotten about justice because there is no such a thing here.

Yet another case. Now is 2007. I know this man. He is about 30 years old but his mind and comprehension is that of maybe a ten year old. But he is a good man and dearly loves children. He is related to my wife and uses to visit for the love of playing with our children. Other than that he loves to walk out and about the township.

So it happened that he was walking about the township and was pressed and needed to use the toilet urgently. In the neighbourhood, in the yard of people known to him and to his family, he entered to use the outside toilet in the corner of a small yard. He opened the toilet without knocking and out and screaming ran a three year old girl to her mother.

Same time the mother opens an attempted rape case. The little girl is taken to the doctor for checkup. The doctor clears the man by declaring that there is no semen, no penetration or whatsoever connected to rape or attempted rape.

I accompany my wife to the police station. No, let me be short.

The next day the man appears before court and he is granted bail. The man is from the poorest of the poor so they have no money for bail. And so the man is remanded in custody.

After three months my wife and I went to pay for the bail of the man and he was released under our care and responsibility. We are supposed to take him back to appear before court on 20 June 2008. Months went by.

19 June 2008. Thursday. Just before sunset we learn that the police have just arrested our man once again. My wife and I rushed to the police station. "What again?" "The same offence and the same charge once again", we are told. "Tomorrow morning we must take him to court for the first case". "No, do not worry we shall take him there," the police woman assures us.

20 June 2008. Friday morning: We rush to the police station to dress him decently and see him off to court at 08h30 in the back of a police van.

20 June 2008. Friday afternoon: Our man is back home. We rushed to the police station to make enquiries. The woman police officer, whose identity is known to us, tells us that she herself arrested him yesterday because of lies and she released him today. We are happy our man is free.

22 June 2008. Sunday evening: A police constable comes to our house to tell us that he has a warrant of arrest for our man. Why? He tells us that it is because our man did not go to court on Friday 20/06/2008.

The police man does not effect arrest and leaves after we explained to him that our man was taken to court by the police on Friday 20/06/2008. We told him that we personally know the police officer who drove our man from police custody on Friday 20/06/2008 to the court.

23 June 2008. Monday morning: The same police constable, also known to us, came to our house again and tells us that there is a little mistake. He takes our man with a promise that he will return him later after correcting the mistake in the court of justice. That was the last time our man saw the sun and breathed fresh air from outside prison walls. He was unjustly put in custody up to today.

I went from pillar to pillar in search of justice. I ended up making a representation before the prosecutors and a magistrate during tea break.

"My Lord, I am . . ."

"Stop! Mense praat Afrikaans in this court."

"Mei . . . . Goood, Ek . . . ek . . . . Please, My Lord, I have very poor command of Afrikaans. Let me speak English please, it is one of the official languages in the new South Africa."

"En so Afrikaans is nie een van hulle nie? Uit my court uit. Die' is nie jou nuwe Suid Afrika nie, is my court, hoor jy, jou . . . jou . . . o-o-r-ge-le-er-de mannetjie. You are over-educated and should be sitting here and I standing there. *Uit!"*

With a loud voice and a bang on the bench I was dismissed, terrified and lonely. Hot Tears came to my eyes and I found myself praying: "God I hate this deployment thing but I wish the President could deploy a comrade and a cadre in each and every court across the country to observe each and every court proceeding and remedy the injustice within 24 hours and report back to him. That shall create 1 000 decent jobs and ease the burden of injustice and pain and suffering and oppression of our people."

We travelled many kilometers by road and lost many thousands of rand in search of justice. We got none. Instead I am still paying a lawyer who promised to take the case for R3000 and then later he multiplied it by several units. He is also Afrikaans speaking white man. When I refused to pay him more than our initial agreed amount, he threatened me with the same court officials to get a garnish order against me. So I am terribly lonely and afraid of our justice and/or injustice courts. So I am paying.

At the rate of this injustice in the house of justice I believe too much injury and injustice had been done to the people, especially the poor. I believe that now is the time for our government to act and stop these evil forces of injustice. Because the mandate of our government is the mandate of ensuring justice and our God is a God of justice. Our President demands justice. Our government must prevent injustice happening in its courts of law, its departments and spheres and including in the private sector were injustice is worse and reigning.

As a matter of urgency the President of the Republic of South Africa must deploy his people and cadres to observe each and every proceedings and dealings in the courts and especially in the private sector. The President of the RSA must also set free hundreds of people who are imprisoned as a result of injustice. Please Mr. President help your people! Deploy comrades and cadres to uproot injustice. Our comrades and cadres shall relieve your people from the flourishing injustice especially in the private sector. Please help Mr. President and Viva!

Mr. President, did you know that at the auction the pricing of cattle, irrespective of the weighting, largely depends on the colour of your skin? The Black people are robbed of their cattle and livestock there. After collecting the little his cattle could make the Black man goes home with no cattle but a heavy broken heart.

I have also been to the auction and last week I realised that this auction system is promoting stock theft from the poor Blacks in many villages. You can come driving cattle or sheep and no questions are asked, no clarification or your ID needed, no brand mark or ear mark or ear tag verified or necessary, the big uncle takes all what you came driving, whether is yours or not, and puts hard cash into your pocket.

After every successful dirty transaction the old big uncle say loud to the other uncle sitting on the opposite side: *"Hoe is die lewe oom?"*

The other uncle replies: *"Die lewe is altyd goed!"*

Then the cattle are loaded in the truck and disappear to where you shall never recover them.

And towards evening my turn came and my cattle were also taken for less than half what they were worth. I went back home with no cattle and instead a heavy bleeding heart.

I went again to other auctions in other provinces and found the same injustice. One other old man protested this robbing business:"I better take back my cattle because you are robbing me off them." The bearded White man in our mist stood up and said: "No, ou Spaanteu, you must let your cattle go because you have no land to take them back to. I told you that from today I no longer want the *(julle) (your)* cattle on my land. *(Julle) koie maak die gras dood* (The Black people's cattle kill the grass) and from next week I shall no longer allow you to stay on my land. *Jy moet nou gaan*! You must go to Mandela Shantytown or Tambo Squatter's Town or Biku (Biko) Village or Mbeki or Sisulo Squatter camp *of enige vuil plek* (or any dirty place)." And then a burst roars of laughter from the stand full of White people.

SHANTYTOWN

Shantytown is nothing
Nothing but a prison
A prison without walls

Shantytown is worse
Worse than a prison
A prison with walls

Ou Spaanteu, single and lonely in the world, blinded by pain of heart, missed the door and walked straight onto the wall. He could have fallen down and hard if it was not of a kind White man who rushed to steady him and led him out from the world of cruelty. The old man was shaking and trembling as if he caught cold in an instant. I came back crying and praying very hard because somehow I knew that ou Spaanteu is gone, spent, and finished.

This is injustice. If you want to *see it naked and all* you only have to dress up in your old greasy overalls and visit the White people's private sectors, there most Whites are openly racist. You must be ready to be called anything including the Ks and *bobbejanne* (monkeys). You must be ready to be sworn at or pushed without provocation. Remember that I have been unjustly suspended with full pay from my government work for nearly a year now. I have got time in my hands and so I started to walk with the poor and market with them. I even worked full day in one good White farmer who treated us like people and a half day in a cruel White farmer who treated us as if we were not people. My experimentation was very captivating, fun and interesting. I will write about it soon. I think you may also go out and have fun and first hand experience. Remember that you must be 100% submissive. Never forget repetition of the words: "*dankie my baas or dankie my miesies*". Never use a single word of English or you shall get into trouble. Very importantly you must think, talk, know and reason far below your level. If you can not cope disappear into the maize fields around ten o' clock during break and call your spouse to pick you up on the nearest main road. It was very frightening and exciting at the same time.

I have experienced and seen and heard of quite a lot of unwarranted injustices and oppression; cruel, unjust, and distressing situations our people are faced with on daily basis.

This episode of injustice and poverty, that continues to punch on us and except praying we remain inactive and helpless, reminds me of my friend in the college many years ago.

Every night before we slept my friend used to pray: "Dear God when you distribute honest beautiful women to honest and crooked men, please save one for me, just one. Amen." And 'Amen' I would say.

My friend would say: "Simon, I think on Sunday we should go to church and maybe we could get honest beautiful girlfriends."

"Why not go to the shopping mall Saturday afternoon buddy?" I asked him.

"Because honest beautiful girls go to church", my friend declared.

"You are correct buddy if you look at it that way. But broadly you are incorrect because bad crooked girls go anywhere." I reasoned.

So I think that this discouraged my friend from searching in the church or anywhere else because twenty years later we met and I found him still saying that same prayer every night and waiting for God to answer. I mean I felt guilty to find him waiting with not a single child on earth, not having a wife, even an ex-wife or a girlfriend-even not a steady one. He is still waiting and waiting and waiting. Waiting and hoping and praying and doing nothing to break free from this suffering.

THE KILLING OF COMRADES MUST STOP!

The killing and harassment of our comrades and cadres must stop! Stop attacking our Councillors and Mayors. Stop stoning them. You must stop stoning and burning their personal properties and possessions. Stop burning our communal properties. Stop! It is wrong. You have missed the point!

You have totally missed the point. Totally without remainder! You have been lied to. You are misled. It is not the Councillor, the Mayor, the MEC, the Premier, the Minister, or the President who are to be blamed. It is the injustice of our possessed possessions. It is the unbroken chains of apartheid that must be blamed. It is the unbroken chains of colonisation that must be blamed. It is the evil of injustice and apartheid consequences that must be blamed, not people! Hands off our people! You must never attack people. You must never kill people. You must never force people to live in fear. It is evil and our God must be angry with us. Stop it!

We have lots of people in government who honestly try to help us out of suffering and poverty. We have lots of people in government who truly feel for the poor. We have lots of people in government who are not corrupt and who fight against corruption. We have people who diligently perform their duties but fail to do little more because their hands are tight by the unbroken chains of apartheid. Hands off our comrades and cadres!

NO LAND FOR GRAZING

Some of the Black people who live in locations and townships still own few cattle and they daily suffer with their cattle in search of grazing. Daily they must suffer as they graze their sheep and cattle alongside busy traffic roads. Together with their cattle they see on both sides of the road endless camps of vacant grazing land which belong to the owner of the land. Together with their livestock they envy the grazing lands which stretch out fallow, vacant and empty. Together with their cattle and sheep they hunger for the abundant grazing in the lands of the owner of the land. Together with their livestock they are tormented by thirst as they see *so near so far* the long and twisting streams of water in the land of the owner of the land.

A bull raises its head and takes a long look at the grazing lands of the owner of the land. A bull bellows and unearthed the grass roots with its front hoofs. It bellowed and unearthed the grass with its horns. It bellowed and took three steps back and suddenly it took a flight clear over the fence and landed safely onto the grazing lands of the owner of the land. Clear and clean it was gone.

The owner of the bull, the poor old man, breaks down into tears. Trying to comfort him I said:"Don't worry, old man, we shall go to the police station and ask the police to help you recover your bull". The old man replies: "I do not cry for the bull. I cry for myself. I only wish I was that bull."

Then I burst into laughter because I remembered the story of "I wish I was that bull" he told me not long ago. He also joined in laughter because surely he remembered it too. Ou Hendrick was like that; full of laughter and when you think he will go north he goes straight south. His story went like this. Growing up he was a very shy person and afraid to propose girls. Mary was

50

about his age and he loved her but could not propose her for years. Almost every time he knew that Mary was alone at their home, he paid her visits but came back without proposing her. One day they were alone at her home, sitting under the shade of a tree. In the middle of a friendly talk the young Hendrick got lost. His mouth was half open and his eyes fixed in the opposite direction to that of Mary. After getting no response from him, Mary shook him back to life. "Hendrick what is it?" Mouthwatering and without thinking he loudly made a declaration: "I wish I was that bull". Mary turned his chair and looked at the opposite direction. Inside the kraal, lo and behold, she saw a bull mounted on top of a cow! And then Mary did something that the young Hendrick never expected. She . . . no, no, I am off the topic. I will write about this one other time. Forgive me for missing the point. The point is: **the land and its wealth must go back to the people!**

NOT EVEN LAND FOR GRAVES

The day of the funeral came. There was a preacher who charged the poor mother double too much to conduct the funeral. The preacher, the man of God, could not do it out of the love of God. The mother paid because her beloved husband deserved a decent funeral.

After service at home the congregation was packed into three open vans and the hearse led the way with the mother to the grave yard 37 kilometers away. "My husband will be very happy to be laid next to his father and mother; there in the grave yard of our forefathers and foremothers," the mother proudly tells the hearse driver.

They arrived back in their land but to their horror there was no grave yard and there were no graves; only a freshly cultivated piece of land. There were no standing remains of walls to prove that people ever lived on this land. The preacher standing next to the mother said: "If I am correct I would say that the arm of the Lord has struck. Or maybe is the new South Africa."

The mother was struck numb with disbelief. She thought that she was dreaming. "No, it can't be true! It must be horrible nightmare and I will awake and find that really it is different. But no I am awake and there are no graves of our past generations. "

Still numb with grief and groaning with heartache the mother cried out loud and clear: "Oh God, where are you? Oh God, do you really care? How can you let this happen to us? Are the graves of our parents also not our possession? Do they also not belong to us? The graves of our parents are gone and missing. We can not live on land and we can not die peacefully on land and we can not be buried on our graveyards next to our parents' graves on land. Our grave yard is destroyed and cultivated and turned into maize fields. Which sin surpasses the erasure of graves from the face of the earth? Graves are a physical connection that connects the living and the dead. It is a continuous relationship between the living and the dead. Death can not destroy the love of the living to the dead. Together—in life and death. To us life is such a whole that not even death can destroy. The continuity that exists between what is seen and not seen. Blessed are those who believe without seeing. To us life is an intrinsic relationship, between the Creator and creature and between the living and the dead, which death can not destroy. Today the hatred and cruelty of the owner of land has done what death can not do. How powerful is the owner of the land!" The mother fainted for the first time in her life.

THE GRAVES

They are sacred
They are revered

In entering the man takes off the hat
In entering the woman puts on the hat
In entering the man and the woman
In entering are silent
In entering steps are calculated
In entering are one
One and together
Together with the unseen

Like at the river Jordan
They kneel down
And confess their trespassing
And plead for their short comings
Give us what we need
And thanks for what we have

For here they know
Are in the gate
Of where they come from
The unknown the unseen
And a man concludes
By leading 'The Lord's prayer'
And the man and the woman says
Amen

THE GRAVEYARD

One day
The orphaned little boy
Runs to the graveyard
After a . . .

Group of little boys
Roasting maize in the fields
The maize field caught fire

The land owner came
Fierce and boiling
Little boys outran him
To the arms of their mothers

The orphaned little boy
With no mother to run to
Ran to the grave yard
Where his mother is buried

The land owner in pursue
The little boy flung himself
Over the rocks covering grave
The land owner tripped
And fell to the other side
He lost his arm and leg
For they were broken
And remained where he fallen
The little boy was whole
Whole and at peace
For when he fling himself
He felt the warmth
The warmth and softness
Of his mother's breast
So death is not the end
But a continuity of life
Of life the other side
Beyond our reasoning
Death is nothing but life after life!

THE FARM KILLINGS MUST STOP!

Farm killings is an act of barbarism and cowardice. It is evil and ungodly. Farm killings that continue in South Africa are a racial killing. The White people, especially Afrikaans speaking, are mercilessly slaughtered in their homes and beds at night. Entire families are exterminated and wiped off as if they are not people made in the image of God. God must be angry where ever He is with these deeds of evil forces.

The land question can not be addressed by killing White people or driving them off to the sea. The land question can not be addressed by dispossessing the Whites of land or driving them away from South Africa. The land question and its wealth must be addressed by equal sharing of land and its wealth to all the people of South Africa.

People who are afraid of change and resist change reason that the inevitable change to land and its wealth ownership shall bring hardships and poverty to South Africa. They reason as if the millions of our people are not already suffering in hardships and poverty. Let me state to them that change to land and its wealth ownership is necessary because millions of our people are already suffering in hardships and poverty.

These people, enemies of the poor, reason that South African currency shall loose its value. So I suggest that our government should not give our enemies a chance to devalue our currency but the government should first stop the use of SA rand and instead use USA dollars or UK pounds. So the devaluing of our currency shall not happen as it happened in Zimbabwe. Our government must know that it can not claim legitimacy unless it is based on the will and wishes of its people. Our government must know that according to the principles of democracy the interests of majority are greater than that of minority. Our government must know that its people have suffered too long in hardships and poverty and now they demand change to land and its wealth ownership.

Also the grabbed wealth of our country which is stocked and invested in over seas countries must be brought back to the motherland. Massive South African wealth, measured in trillions of pounds, is over seas in the hands of private ownership; individuals and corporate. Some of this ownership has in their possession our gold. Some of these super power countries have gold reserves; reserves of gold which was stolen during the grabbing of our land and its wealth. These countries control the value of South African gold, platinum, diamond, rand, and everything. They continue to live at ease and we continue to live and die in poverty. I write these so that you should realise that it is not fair to target White farmers as if they took everything from the poor. White farmers must only share land with Black people and help Black people to get back South African massive wealth from over seas. The White people also deserve a share of the stolen South African wealth in overseas. They are our people and partners in search of better life for all. The farm killings must stop! The racial killings must stop! Evil deeds of cowardice and barbarism must stop! It is not African to kill women and children. Our ancestors must be angry at us and ashamed of us where ever they are. STOP killing White people! It is evil and ungodly. Stop it!

From where I am standing I can see a better South Africa in not so far a distant tomorrow. At the horizon I can see a South Africa of true change, true peace and true reconciliation. I can see a South Africa of contended people living without guilt, fear, hatred, anger, injustice, and poverty. I can almost feel, smell and touch the future; the future of our beloved South Africa! I humbly call the government of South Africa and its entire people to get into a peaceful march and march into the future of prosperity. Dr. Martin Luther King says: "Take the first step in faith. You do not have to see the whole staircase. Just take the first step."

THE KILLING OF
FOREIGNERS MUST STOP!

Killing of foreigners is an act of barbarism and cowardice. It is evil and ungodly. Foreigner killing that continues in South Africa is ethnic killing. The African people, especially from Zimbabwe, are mercilessly slaughtered in their homes and beds at night. Entire families are exterminated and wiped off as if they are not people made in the image of God. God must be angry where ever He is with these deeds of evil forces.

The question of poverty can not be addressed by killing African people or driving them off to the sea. The poverty question and unemployment can not be addressed by killing other people. Poverty and unemployment must be addressed by equal sharing of land and its wealth to all the people of South Africa.

People who are afraid of change and resist change reason that the inevitable change to land and its wealth ownership shall bring hardships and poverty to South Africa. They reason as if the millions of our people are not already suffering in hardships and poverty. Let me state to them that change to land and its wealth ownership is necessary because millions of our people are suffering in hardships and poverty.

These people, enemies of the poor, reason that South African currency shall loose its value. So I suggest that our government should not give our enemies a chance to devalue our currency but the government should first stop the use of SA rand and instead use USA dollars or UK pounds. So the devaluing of our currency shall not happen as it happened with Zimbabwe. Our government must know that it can not claim legitimacy unless it is based on the will and wishes of its people. Our government must know that according to the principles of democracy the interests of majority are greater than that of minority. Our government must know that its people have suffered too long in hardships and poverty and now they demand change to land and its wealth ownership.

Also the grabbed wealth of our country which is stocked and invested in over seas countries must be brought back to the motherland. Massive South African wealth, measured in billions of pounds, is over seas in the hands of private ownership; individuals and corporate. Some of this ownership has in their possession our gold. Some of these super power countries have gold reserves; reserves of gold which was stolen during the grabbing of our land and its wealth. These countries control the value of South African gold, platinum, diamond, rand, and everything. They continue to live at ease and we continue to live and die in poverty. I write these so that you should realise that it is not fair to target other Africans as if they are the cause of our troubles, hardships and our suffering in poverty. Africa is Africa and an African is African as you and me. Irrespective of apartheid borders, an African is an African! Please take note that the people of Zimbabwe (although not all) are the descendants of our people who were under Chief Mzilikazi. Chief Mzilikazi, the former Zulu warrior under King Shaka of the mighty Zulu people. They lived together with us in South Africa before the Whites made the land too hot for us. Chief Mzilikazi and his people fled us behind and went on northwards and terrorised the BaShona people in Bashonaland (now Zimbabwe) and captured their land. They named the stolen Bashonaland the Matabeleland. Later the Whites captured the land from the Matebele (Matebeleland). They named the stolen land Rhodesia. And now President Mugabe has captured back their own land (the land of the Shona) from the Matebele (descendants of Shaka Zulu) and the White people. He named it Zimbabwe. And now President Mugabe has made the land too hot for both the Matebele and the Whites. The Matebele people fled back to South Africa because it is the land of their origin and ancestors. South Africa is the land of their roots! They are our people and partners in search of better life. After all the present borders are the borders of colonisation and apartheid. The killings of Zimbabweans must stop! They are also people! They are one with us. We share common ancestry. The ethnic killings must stop! Evil deeds of cowardice and barbarism must stop! It is not African to kill women and children. Our ancestors must be angry with us and ashamed of us where ever they are. STOP killing foreigners! It is evil and ungodly.

Stop it!

About the Whites arriving to capture Matebeleland, Wilbur Smith, in his book "Men of Men", writes: "Each day they come up the road to Thaba Induna, and they bring their tawdry gifts and the little green bottles of madness. Their words are as sweet as honey on the tongue, but they catch in the throat of those who try to swallow them as though they were the green bile of the crocodile. This one asks for the right to hunt elephant and take the teeth, this one asks for the young girls to be sent to his wagon, another wants to tell the nation about a strange white god, another wishes to dig a whole and look for the yellow iron, yet another wishes to buy cattle. One says he wants only this, and another only that, but they want it all. These people are consumed by a hunger that can never be appeased, they burn with a thirst that can never be assuaged. They want everything they see, and even that is never enough for them. They take the very earth, but that is not enough, so they tear it open like a man tearing a child from the mother's womb. They take the rivers, and that is not enough, so they build walls across them and turn them into lakes. They ride after the elephant herds and shoot them down, not just one or two, not just the big bulls, but all of them—the breeding cows and the calves with ivory no longer than your finger. Everything they see they take; and they see everything, for they are always moving and searching and looking."

POLICE ABUSE MUST STOP!

Police men and women are our brothers and sisters
It is wrong to use them on the front line
On the front line against men and women
Men and women who still suffer the evils of apartheid
The evils of apartheid the police also suffer from
People marching and protesting
Marching and protesting for water
For electricity, for houses
For toilets, for roads
For schools, for clinics
For life and tired of dead living
Are not criminals
People marching and occupying the vacant land
The vacant motherland in Cape Town
Are not criminals
Because is not a crime and it can never be a crime
To demand back your possessed possessions
So it is wrong to treat them as criminals
Criminals are those who treat them as criminals
Stop police abuse by stopping to use them against what
They know is correct and is a right
Stop police abuse by stopping to think for them
Thinking for them as if they have no brains
And an inborn sense of what is right and what is wrong
Stop abuse by stopping to turn them into public enemies
You can not solve social and economic injustices
In South Africa by sacrificing our brothers and sisters
By sacrificing the police, but by directly addressing
The question of possessed possessions

POLICE KILLINGS MUST STOP!

Stop killing our police officers
They are our brothers and sisters
Stop killing our police officers
They are the victims of abuse on the police system
They are the victims of public misdirected vengeance
Vengeance arising from the continuing suffering
Suffering of injustice arising from the unbroken chains
The unbroken chains of apartheid
Stop the killing of police because they are the victims
The victims of circumstances
The victims that suffer double sacrificial victimisation
Stop killing our police officers because they are caught
They are caught between two devils
They personally suffer the unbroken chains of apartheid
They are forced to act against their wishes
Their wishes of breaking the unbroken chains of apartheid
They are forced to act against the people marching
The people marching against what they do not wish
The people marching against what they do not want
The people marching against the injustices of apartheid
The people marching against the unbroken chains of apartheid
Hands off our POLICE!
Let them march with the people!
Let them march to South Africa!
South Africa of True Change and Equality!
South Africa of NO possessed possessions!
South Africa of Blacks and Whites as equals in entirety!

THE CONSTITUTION
AND DEMOCRACY

The constitution of a democratic country must allow that the welfare of majority be greater than that of minority. It must be seen to advance the welfare of majority. I think that there is something wrong with our constitution or our democracy because we are stuck.

I think our constitution is based on principles of false democracy which protect the welfare and interests of minority at the expense and much injury to the majority.

It is a big mistake to allow the constitutional court and other courts in South Africa to continue operating supremely and subverting political power because political power is the only power at this stage in the hands of the multitudes of South Africans.

It is very wrong to continue allowing that political disputes resulting from the exercise of powers constitutionally conferred upon the ANC through majority vote be sabotaged by the courts. In his book President Nelson Mandela writes: "The ANC has not struggled against apartheid only to yield to a disguise form of it. We cannot allow for the bringing back of apartheid through the back door".

Ntate Zuma, the President of the people and RSA, made a brilliant and intellectual observation by declaring that: "The powers conferred on the courts cannot be superior to the powers resulting from the political and consequently administrative mandate resulting from popular democratic elections." Our President is correct!

Those who own the things that people must have strongly differ with the President. Viva Mr. President! Now "Take the first step in faith. You need not see the whole staircase." Overwhelming majority of our people agrees with you and they have already given you their vote! God agrees with you because He is a God of justice!

THE ULTIMATE SOLUTION FOR SOUTH AFRICA

THE MODEL OF ROOTING OUT POVERTY

Step 1

The government must come up with a new Land Act that honestly and openly addresses the injustice of 1913 and 1936 Land Acts. This New Land Act must earnestly seek to advance the Black people to a little more equal footing with the Whites. Economic equal standing must now be accorded to both Black and White people. 1994 only gave us political equal standing which is meaningless without economic freedom.

After the Anglo-Boer war (1899-1902), Hertzog came with 'the two stream' policy based on the principle that reconciliation of the English and Afrikaans people was only possible if equal footing and equal standing was accorded to both groups. It was an effort to bring equality between two groups so that they could exist as equal partners and live in peace (S.F. Malan et al, 202). And Hertzog was correct, it worked out successfully.

The New Land Act must be based on the above accession and on the fact that war has already been fought; blood already been shed; graves already been dug and closed; war has already been won and lost; and thousands of freedom fighters already been buried in the battle field;—for the struggle of this land and its wealth, that rightfully belongs to the Blacks and Whites of this country; not to the Whites only.

We do not need war because it has passed and ended years back. It ended with Mandela's vote and De Klerk's vote. It ended with your vote and my vote in 1994.

We shall not and never again take up arms and turn South Africa into a battle field. We love this country and its people. We are neighbours; in a real sense Blacks and Whites are neighbours. This makes us one. So the prospect of civil war does not exist. It is impossible. There is no room for self slaughtering and self destruction in our beloved South Africa of after 1994.

Today, God willing and God on the side of all South Africans—both Black and White—let us all declare that there shall be no civil war in our time and the time after us because we do justice. Because we are laying concrete foundations for future generations based on the will and love of God. So that we all leave this land a better place where God's children shall all reap and enjoy the fruit of the land together and equally. Let it be.

Step 2

The New Land Act must awaken up the owners of the land to reality so that they willingly and rightfully give back half of land to the people of South Africa. By giving back half each remains with the other half and clear conscience, peace, and security. To uproot people from land is cruel and evil so it must be avoided at all costs. I write a big NO to the killing and uprooting of White farmers from the land; let them keep half and continue with farming and production. They are our brothers and sisters and we need them. At this stage the White farmers give back half of land to the government of South Africa.

Step 3

Now half of the land is in the hands of government. There are many options at this stage. Let me come with only one. Any how, at this stage you shall be allowed to make submissions of other better options.

Step 4

The government stops from being a parasite without producing. The department of farming and production is created, with its full ministry and budget allocation. This department must concentrate on massive production of dairy products, poultry, beef, mutton, pork, crops, vegetables and all kinds of fruits. Massive production shall help to bring down prices so that the poor can afford to feed their children. The aim of this department is to offer job opportunities to the hundred thousands of the poor; to eradicate hunger and to do away with monthly food parcels and social grants from the government.

Millions of rand are used to purchase livestock from each land owner. Other millions are used to lease farming equipment from the land owner on annual basis. Millions are set aside to employ knowledge and skills of each land owner as superintend on the government land. This makes him a partner and a friend of the people; one with the people; a true South African. The walls of fear and insecurity and hatred are pulled down, never to be built up again. S/he represents the government on land and is responsible to ensure the success of this model.

The government appoints deputy superintend for each farm. These persons are also very key and fundamental to the success or failure of the whole model. They should not be deployed politicians. They must be appointed on merit. They must be hardworking people dedicated and committed to sweat for the success of this model. Always ready and willing to take instructions from the superintendent. To sustain good working relationship with the superintendent. To develop this working relationship to the level of friendship. Willing and eager to live and stay in the government house on land. She/he is a connection between the land and the government. Deputy superintend is contracted for a five year period and it can be extended based on his relations with his/her immediate senior.

Step 5

The Superintend and his or her deputy work hand in hand and in earnest and honesty to see the success of South Africa. Abandoned farming lands must be in use once again. We need them more than ever before. The two government officials plan together. Which land is suitable for settlement? How many families can be allocated land for settlement? How big the yard should be? Which land for cultivation? Which for dairy farming? How many jobs created in dairy farming? How many jobs created in crop farming? How many jobs created in poultry? How many learners the closed school can enroll? How many teaching jobs are created? How many jobs for support staff at the school? How big the government trading store should be? How many jobs can it create? Which basics can it sell? How shall it be administered? When is mobile clinic needed? Running water and electricity must be accessible to people who come to settle on land. Transport system must also be available. Farm settlements must be planned and must look like small towns, with paved streets, lights and running water. The government must build beautiful farm town houses with not less than three bedrooms which shall attract teachers, doctors, nurses, church ministers and other professionals to go and live in farm towns. The farm labourers also reside in these same farm town houses, the father and the mother club together in paying monthly loan installments for the house they live in. The loan repayment is spread over a period of years depending on how much they earn. After loan is paid off the houses belong to the people. The right of decent ownership is restored.

Our government must stop building prisons worth 100 millions of rand. Our government must stop building RDP shelters in smallest pieces of land known as "RDP houses". "RDP houses" build without a room for privacy, not the privacy you think of but a small toilet build right inside the kitchen with walls half way to the roof. What indecency! Our government must stop social grants worth millions of rand to the poor. Our government must stop with monthly food parcels. The above savings of money must be used in developing farm towns. The over seas stock markets and countries must give back the wealth that amounts to trillions of UK pounds that rightly belong to South Africa and its people. Gold reserves in the foreign countries rightly belong to South Africa and its people. The AngloGold, Anglo American and Anglo Platinum must now plough back into the lives of the dispossessed rightful owners of South African mines. UK and Europe must compensate South African Blacks for death and destruction of their livelihood they suffered during colonisation spearheaded by Britain. Trillions of pounds in compensation to South Africa must wash our hands. The last resort is the World Bank and IMF. These banks were available to help apartheid South Africa with loans in the destruction of people's lives. I am sure they shall be happy and readily available in helping democratic South Africa with loans in the building of people's lives. The time is now to build a new South Africa! No room for postponements and delays because the sun cannot wait, my son cannot wait, thirst, and hunger cannot be postponed.

Let us break for air. Tell me what is in the name. Why? Africa is the major producer of mineral wealth but I only read about AngloGold in South Africa as if our gold is from England and I also read about Anglo-American gold in South Africa as if our gold is from England and America. In Africa we have BP (British Petroleum) and no AP (African Petroleum). Is there no oil in Africa? In America our Black people are called African Americans and not Americans but our gold is called American Gold not African. Why our Blacks are classified as African Americans not Americans *finish en klaar*? In South Africa the Whites must be called South Africans not American Africans, England Africans, German Africans, Holland Africans, or Dutch Africans. Why they are not called Americans or British? Why they are not called Germans or Dutch or Hollanders but Afrikaners (Africans)? Why they are not called Germans as Indians are called Indians in South Africa? Did you know that "Afrikaans taal" ("African language") and English are not African but originate from overseas? Gold, platinum, oil and wealth originate in Africa although they use overseas names for them. There must be something in the name more than my eyes can see. I am trying to figure it out but I cannot put my finger on it. So let us continue.

Hundred thousands of poverty stricken families willingly move back to live and work in farm towns and rightfully occupy the motherland. Locations and townships and towns and cities are cleared off of squatter camps and shantytowns. The municipalities get back the land vacated and space to breath. The war at the dumping sites ends as they clear off. The lists for social grants and RDP houses and needs and sanitation and running water and electricity become shorter and shorter and come to a dead end as people willingly move back to occupy motherland and make self-sufficient livelihoods on their motherland.

Families moving back are monthly paid decently by the department from funds generated by farming and massive production. They must be paid well enough so that they can build or purchase their own farm town houses and develop their own estates. They own their own farm town houses with small vegetable gardens and fruit trees around their yards. They are allowed to buy and own few cattle for children to drink milk and for insurance in times of misfortune. They must be allowed to keep few hens for Sunday meal. And lastly they must be allowed to keep a pig or two for slaughtering in winter. This means that one camp (piece of land) must be kept aside for communal use in each and every farm town. Do not worry about overgrazing because after each and every harvest food for livestock shall be in oversupply and stored for the times of need. So there shall be no overgrazing.

Now that people work and earn their living they become more human and bigger and dignified. They feel deep satisfaction and protection and inner peace to spread to others; because a human being is born with a right to work the land, right to own and control animals, right to love the land and right to live and be happy on the land.

People become whole and live once again after centuries of dead living. At this stage the heavens and the holy communion of our ancestors and angels are singing hallelujahs and glory to God the almighty! Now that we have strived to allow the will of God happen on earth (at least in South Africa) as it is in heaven, our people shall be blessed beyond human comprehension. High rate of crime slowly dies out and delivery protests are no more. The threat of revolts or to overthrow our government disappears never to appear again. People are people again! They live without fear, hatred and poverty! They have opportunity to love, work and play in absolute safety. In the morning the father wakes up with a tune in his lips. Hunger is gone and children play in love and laughter for the whole day. In the evening after hot shower children are tired, they hurry to bed and fall asleep in 90 seconds. In the evening the mother prepares dinner with that harmonious praise hymn: **Modimo wa boikanyo**. Glory is to God!

NO ROOM FOR WAR

In a war all are not winners
In a war all are real losers
Even the winner is not real
He is a loser
All are losers because all
All have lost something
Something and someone
Someone fallen
Fallen never to rise up again
Fallen where he stood
Where he stood for
For a bloody stinking war
No winners but wimping losers
All their victories add up to far less
To far less than what they could have gained
Without war

ONLY A MANSION FOR PEACE

How beautiful you are
Like a bride in the morn of ululations
Sweet like a heart of water melon
Serene like a child on mother's breast
Contented like a lotto winner
True peace how just, fair and noble you are!

Blessed are those who know you
Who seek and dwell in you
Who water your tree
And dwell on its shade

Peace the innocent and just
How proper you are
How fair and just you must be
To knit up worn out human relations
To seal bleeding relative wounds
To balm hurt family relations
And glue loose marriage ties
The knot that ties siblings together
The chief nourishment of prosperity
The spring, the fountain, the very source of our life

How inseparable you are
With love and justice
Peace, love and justice together
Together are strong and infinite
Peace without the two limps
Only brittles and fleeting a ways
Peace that stands endlessly
Is corner stoned and locked
On truth, love and justice

CONCLUSION

People have been waiting from 1994 for true change and better life for all. The poor shall tell you that they are still waiting for freedom and equality and democracy. They shall confess to you that they think that if this thing is democracy then it is worse than apartheid. People shall tell you that they are still waiting for change. The poor shall tell you that there is no new South Africa; all that is new is the colour of the President of the Republic of South Africa.

I know many of us, who have decent paying jobs; who have comfortable big houses and properties; who own more than one car; who live in towns and cities; who have the things people must have; who are propitious; argue against the view held by the majority of our people and we want to maintain the status quo in the interest of our good life and investments and save margins. While on the other hand great majority of our people are born into poverty and die in extreme poverty.

Auspicious people who hold wealth of the country in their hands celebrate when they see our people shifting focus from the land and its wealth to government and its scarce resources. They celebrate when they see our people wasting time, energy, and their lives over tenders and positions in municipalities and provinces. They celebrate when they see our people getting divided.

They celebrate when they see former comrades becoming fierce enemies up in arms. They celebrate when they see us moving steadfast into loggerheads. Into war that shall be called Black on Black violence. Brothers and sisters killing each other over little piece of cake in the government hands, oblivious of the whole cake in the hands of private ownership and totally forgetting people who wrongly own things that people must have. We do not need war, we do not want war. The oppressed people, Black people, irrespective of political affiliation, must be united more than ever before. Black on black violence that erupted in the 1990s cost us too much. Without it our icon Nelson Mandela and other freedom fighters could have then gained economic freedom for us. We lost it and gained political freedom without economic freedom.

People who own things that people must have celebrate when we blame the results as the causes of suffering and poverty in South Africa. They want us to blame crime and corruption and tender-preneur and HIV/Aids and protests and strikes as causes of suffering and poverty in South Africa. It is not true. They are the results not causes. They are the results of established and legalised poverty of the great majority of South Africans.

A desperate girl ends up contracting HIV as a result of living in dire poverty. People who are lazy to think deep might think that I promote HIV and the above wrongs. No, I do not promote them. They are wrong. But take note that they are only leaves and branches. Do not waste time on leaves and branches. Go straight to the root. Uproot the tree. Uproot poverty. Address poverty directly. Give back land and its wealth to the people.

The land and wealth of this country is enough to sustain its entire people to lead a better life without dying in poverty.

God forbids that we, the people of South Africa, should continue to allow the rich and the powerful to exploit the masses of our poor Black people by turning them into beasts of burden to carry investor interests and the interests of economic stability, growth, and prosperity which they do not enjoy. There is no opening for them to enjoy the products of their toil and hard labour but continue to suffer and die in dire poverty.

From where I am standing I can see a better South Africa in not so far a distant tomorrow. At the horizon I can see a South Africa of true change, true peace and true reconciliation. I can see a South Africa of contended people living without guilt, fear, hatred, anger, injustice, and poverty. I can almost feel, smell and touch the future; the future of our beloved South Africa! I humbly call upon the government of South Africa and its entire people to get into a peaceful march and march into the future of prosperity.

Dr. Martin Luther King says: "Take the first step in faith. You do not have to see the whole staircase. Just take the first step."

I humbly call upon the foreign markets, corporate and countries which benefited massive South African wealth before apartheid, during apartheid and after apartheid to please help us out of poverty. Poverty, hunger and lack are finishing us off. We are dead without your help. Please help the government and the people of South Africa. In Matthews Jesus Christ says: "I verily tell you, whenever you helped the poor, you helped me. I verily tell you, whenever you helped one of my poor brothers and sisters, you did it for me!"

In advance I pray that may God bless you and guide you as you think of helping South Africa and its people. Amen.

MATSIME SIMON MOHAPI

Sebata, tebetebe e e mohahla o logong
Sebata, tshehla ka nala tsa tshipi
Sebata, tau e e mahlo a maribitla
Sebata, lepeke lekalla la maboea bofubedu!

Lebang Mohapi ka mahlong o maribitla
Ha a maribitla ke mahlo a tau
Ke motaung ke motho o borra Thulo M'phete
Motho o borra Mosunye—Tebetebe ea ha Moletsane
Motsalwa ke Kgasa le Pulane Mmita Mohapi
Mohapi ea tsamayang a hapa dipelo tsa makau le
makgarebe; o ka ba oare Modimo o mo theositse hore
Batho ba tsebe thato ea Modimo lefatsheng!

Helehelele bomme le bontate!
Kana tau ga e tsomiwe e se mmutlanyana
Mogatsa motsoma tau o batla seantlo go sale gale
Ka ditlameloana tsa pula di baakanngwa go sale gale!

Mohapi ke motaung o na oa ha esale
Ke tau e e kileng eare e poruma sekgweng
Banna makwala ba hlanola direthe le ka mahlo ba sa e
bona ba utlwile modumo e poruma! Lefatshe la
thothomela ke modumo oa tau ha e poruma!
Poruma Mohapi lefatshe le tle le utlwe!
Poruma o kgobole ka kodu! Hapi le ka pene o kgobole
O kgobole le mo go sa kgobogeng teng go kgoboge!

Kgobola Mohapi kgobola go kgoboge
Kgobola o bule tsela bana ba batho ba bone tsela
Bula tsela bana ba chabana sa Rrantsho ba tle ba goroge
Ba goroge fatsheng la boswa jwa bona
Fatsheng le ba le a betsweng ke Modimo
Ba le amogwa ka dikgoka le ka tshollo ya madi
Kgobola Tau, kgobola Sebata, kgobola Mohapi
Setshaba se tle se boelwe ke lefatshe le khumo ya sona!

Mohapi ke sebata ke tsehla ea dikgwa
Ka mahlo a a tukang malakabe, malakabe a malakabe
Malakabe a mollo oa lerato, lerato la sechaba sa Afrika!
Poruma moseka phofu ya ga gabo ga ake a swa lentswe!
Mohapi ke tau e e kileng ya re e tsena ka motse
Banna ba sia ba palama matlo ka hodimo
Basadi ba kena tlase ha dibete!
Ya feta tau ya itlhabela petsana tse pedi ka sakeng la
Morena ea ja ea kgora ha e fetsa ea kgobola
Ya re e kgobola dithota le dipoa tsa a rabela
Ha ba ha hlaha lentswe lehodimong la botsa
La botsa hore ho senyehile eng tlase lefatsheng
Ba araba ba re: "Ke Tau, Ke Tshehla, Ke Sebata,
Ke Mohapi, motho o' rra Mosunye, O feditse!"
Ka namane e thala e khuhlela mosehlelong! Helehelele!
Dumang, MaAfrika porumang, porumang
Porumang ka moporo o mogolo
Lo etse fa dinku di lelela dikonyana
Porumang ka lentswe le legolo
Jaaka loseka phofu, lefatshe le khumo ya lona.
Kana moseka phofu ya ga gabo ga a ke a swa lentswe! Porumang
MaAfrika go be go utlwagale. Porumang! Dumang Badimo ba kgatlhege!
Pula! Nala! Khotso!